A Family Just Like Mine

Barbara-Anne Puren

First published in Great Britain by Springtime Books 2018

Copyright © Barbara-Anne Puren

All rights reserved. No part of this publication may be reproduced, stored in or introduced into a retrieval system or transmitted, in any form, or by any means (electronic, mechanical, photocopying, recording or otherwise) without the prior written permission from the publisher.

This book is sold subject to the condition that it shall not, by way of trade or otherwise, be lent, resold, hired out or otherwise circulated without the publisher's proper consent in any form of binding or cover other than in which it is published and without a similar condition including this condition being imposed on the subsequent purchaser.

ISBN: 978-0-9955027-9-6

Illustrations by Barbara-Anne Puren

Designed by author2author (www.author2author.co.uk)

Springtime
Books

Dedicated to my daughter Cassidy and my husband Vic
– for always and forever it will be.

With thanks to my husband Vic as well as Valérie Besanceney, Jo and Joshua Parfitt and of course my much-loved family and friends who supported and encouraged me to write this book.

Contents

Foreword

We all have different families, and each is special because it is unique. Not one family is 'normal' except that it is normal to be unique. Every family has its ups and downs, its challenges and its celebrations. As *A Family Just Like Mine* beautifully explains, the single most important thing is that we love each other and support each other through it all.

As a teacher, I come across all kinds of families and it always warms my heart when a child proudly describes his or her family. At a young age, children are usually unabashedly proud of their families, no matter what the set-up is. That is the way it should be. However, sometimes, when children share their family situation on the playground, they are met with disbelief or denial ("you cannot have two mummies, that isn't possible"). We are all often left with questions when presented with unfamiliar situations, but at a young age, children are not yet equipped to explain why their family is just as normal and possible as any other.

In *A Family Just Like Mine*, Barbara-Anne Puren helps children understand that there are many different definitions of a family. Many children will recognize their own families portrayed in this story. By the end, they will hopefully have gained a newfound appreciation and understanding for their peers who may have families different from their own, but are bound by love.

Thank you, Gemma, for being so wonderfully inquisitive and taking us on your adventurous journey looking for a family just like yours. We can all learn from your open-minded and curious attitude. You help children (and adults) understand, with compassion and kindness, to acknowledge all families just the way they are.

Valérie Besanceney, International School Primary Teacher and Author of B at Home: Emma Moves Again and My Moving Booklet.

www.valeriebesanceney.com

Chapter One

Gemma Leaves Home

One day, not so very long ago, a young girl called Gemma decided to go on a journey. This was no ordinary journey. It was a journey that not many nine-year-old girls are brave enough to go on.

You see, Gemma, like each and every one of you, was a very special child. What made her so special was that she was extremely inquisitive. She would search and search until she found the perfect answer to a question – even if she had to travel the world in order to find it.

Now, Gemma didn't want her dearest mommy and daddy to worry about her while she was gone. But, as she was not quite sure how long her journey would take, she decided to write a letter telling them what she was about to do.

Oops, I almost forgot to mention it! The other very special thing about Gemma was that she loved to rhyme. Do you know how to rhyme? Do you?

If I say: CAT   You say: MAT

If I say: BLUE   You say: SHOE

If I say: PUDDLE   You say: MUDDLE

If I say: BEE   You say: TREE

If I say: DOG   You say: FROG

To My Dearest Mommy and Daddy

I'm going on a journey, see,

To find a special FAMILY.
Now please don't worry and please don't cry,
I have to go and you know why.

I've started a search throughout the earth,
For this FAMILY I must find.
I'll explore every inch for all its worth,
For a FAMILY that's just like mine.

Mom, don't worry, I'll wear my coat,
When it's hot I'll wear sunscreen too.
Dad, you'll be glad that I've got pound notes,
I'll bring home some chocolates for you.

With all my love, from your daughter Gemma. Xxx

So she packed tasty treats safely into her bag
And began to sing her own song.
Not forgetting to pack her best teddy called Scraggs,
For company while she was gone.

Then she took a big step just outside her front door –
Her amazing journey began.
She would travel the world just to search and explore,
While she hopped, she skipped and she sang.

"I'm looking for a FAMILY,
I wonder what I'll find?
I'm looking for a FAMILY
That will be just like mine."

Chapter Two
The Family at Number 15

The first FAMILY she found were at number 15,
In a house on the very same street.
With an upstairs and downstairs and yard that was clean,
This FAMILY, they looked so complete.

There was Mommy and Daddy and baby boy too,
Who giggled and played with dear Scraggs,
And she found them so sweet, this first FAMILY, who,
By meeting them made her HEART glad.

Well, HIGH FIVE is a great way to greet.
HIGH FIVE – it's a cool thing to do.
Just HIGH FIVE to your friends on the street.
It's fun to HIGH FIVE, can you?

Gemma saw they were happy, this FAMILY of three,
As they cuddled and played with their son,
And even dear Scraggs was content as can be –
Gemma's HEART was most easily won.

But she needed to know and to just understand,
Since this was the reason she came,
She needed to know how this FAMILY began –
So she played the TUMMY HEART GAME!

"There is this thing I'm thinking of,
It might sound strange and funny,
But just where are your children from?
Your HEART or from your TUMMY?"

"I hope my question's not too hard,
But I'd like to know, you see,
Is your FAMILY TUMMY or HEART?
Please say if they're just like me."

Both the mom and the dad gently stroked baby's head,
He was sweeter than any she'd seen.
"He is from my TUMMY," the mom softly said,
And they smiled. They looked so serene.

Though she liked them a lot their great answer was not
The one that she needed to hear,
So the time had now come, Gemma had to move on,
And search for that FAMILY, so dear.

Without further ado, in her HEART Gemma knew,
That she must take her search high and low.
So she boarded a boat as her confidence grew,
And sang as she started to row.

"I'm looking for a FAMILY,
I wonder what I'll find?
I'm looking for a FAMILY
That will be just like mine."

Chapter Three
Jumping in Anglesey

Now, just over the sea lived a new FAMILY,
With two moms but not with a dad.
They made friends magically, on the isle Anglesey
Where they lived with their little dog Madge.

Now, their girl was called Eve, and their boy they called Frog!
Though his real name was actually Rhawn,
And he loved to be tickled and play with the dog,
While he jumped up and down on the lawn.

Well, JUMP is Frog's favourite game.
JUMP – it's his best thing to do.
Just Frog JUMP, it's like his name.
It's fun to Frog JUMP, can you?

Just two moms and no dad with two children so neat,
Gemma really liked jumping along,
And she thought them a treat and the dog hard to beat;
They had fun as they sang her song.

But she needed to know and to just understand,
Since this was the reason she came,
She needed to know how this FAMILY began –
So she played the TUMMY HEART GAME!

"There is this thing I'm thinking of,
It might sound strange and funny,
But just where are your children from?
Your HEART or from your TUMMY?"

"I hope my question's not too hard,
But I'd like to know, you see,
Is your FAMILY TUMMY or HEART?
Please say if they're just like me."

Then together as one with no need to translate,
They smiled and nodded their heads.
The moms shouted out "TUMMY!" which Eve thought was great,
While Frog jumped right over their legs!

Though she liked them a lot their great answer was not
The one that she needed to hear,
So the time had now come, Gemma had to move on,
And search for that FAMILY, so dear.

She leapt over the gate then jumped in the air,
She giggled and waved them goodbye.
It was harder than finding a diamond so rare,
This FAMILY she needed to find.

"I'm looking for a FAMILY,
I wonder what I'll find?
I'm looking for a FAMILY
That will be just like mine."

Chapter Four

Greeting Giants in Bolivia

Gemma hopped on a plane bound for Bolivia,
It did not take so very long,
Where a FAMILY of giants said "Jay! Welcome dear."
They were friendly, so big and so strong!

She looked up at the parents, their shoulders so broad –
They even had super-sized feet!
"Come and meet our two girls." This left Scraggs over-awed:
"They're almost as tall as a tree!"

Well, STRETCH up as high as you can.
STRETCH – now pretend to be huge.
Just STRETCH, striding over the land.
It's fun to STRETCH up high, can you?

Giant mom and the dad and two girls, I must add,
Were delightful right from the start.
And so there in Bolivia good times Gemma had.
This big FAMILY warmed up her HEART.

But she needed to know and to just understand,
Since this was the reason she came,
She needed to know how this FAMILY began –
So she played the TUMMY HEART GAME!

"There is this thing I'm thinking of,
It might sound strange and funny,
But just where are your children from?
Your HEART or from your TUMMY?"

"I hope my question's not too hard,
But I'd like to know, you see,
Is your FAMILY TUMMY or HEART?
Please say if they're just like me."

Then the mom and the dad, they talked and made tea,
Munching toast with Bolivian honey.
Both their daughters agreed and they shouted with glee,
"We came from this giant mommy's TUMMY!"

Though she liked them a lot their great answer was not
The one that she needed to hear,
So the time had now come, Gemma had to move on,
And search for that FAMILY, so dear.

Then they all hugged goodbye as she jumped on a train,
Giant tears welling up in their eyes.
Then she hopped on a plane, on her journey again,
And she sang as she took to the skies.

"I'm looking for a FAMILY,
I wonder what I'll find?
I'm looking for a FAMILY
That will be just like mine."

Chapter Five

Greenland's Doggy Delights

Next, she landed in Greenland, the light was so bright,
She thought it was so very strange.
For although it's called 'Green' it was covered in ice,
She needed someone to explain!

And then just when she thought there was no one around,
To her greatest surprise and delight,
A new FAMILY was found, with a whole pack of hounds,
Now, this was a wonderful sight.

For the FAMILY she saw had one dad and one mom,
Three children and toddler, too cute!
But this next part was new 'cause their dogs filled the room,
How they romped, how they snuggled and chewed!

Well, SKATE on the ice in the snow.
SKATE – with dogs pulling sleds too.
Just SKATE shouting "Hike!" so they go.
It's fun to ice SKATE, can you?

With this FAMILY unique, in the snow and the sleet,
With their dogs that howled and barked,
When they cuddled together their life was complete,
And Gemma was glad to take part.

But she needed to know and to just understand,
Since this was the reason she came,
She needed to know how this FAMILY began –
So she played the TUMMY HEART GAME!

"There is this thing I'm thinking of,
It might sound strange and funny,
But just where are your children from?
Your HEART or from your TUMMY?"

"I hope my question's not too hard,
But I'd like to know, you see,
Is your FAMILY TUMMY or HEART?
Please say if they're just like me."

Then the mom and the dad answered one and the same,
"Our children came from Mom's TUMMY,
But the dogs aren't the same," as they joined in the game,
"They came from their own doggy mummy!"

Though she liked them a lot their great answer was not
The one that she needed to hear,
So the time had now come, Gemma had to move on,
And search for that FAMILY, so dear.

Gem and Scraggs had to leave, so she hugged them all tight,
Especially the dogs, who were fun.
Goodbye to this land with the sun at midnight,
Time to go – it was time to move on.

"I'm looking for a FAMILY,
I wonder what I'll find?
I'm looking for a FAMILY
That will be just like mine."

Chapter Six
Sliding Down Sand Dunes in Egypt

Then she rode on a camel, a great way to travel,
To Egypt, a mysterious land.
With the tales of its pyramids all to unravel,
And tall Sphinxes, covered in sand.

There was a FAMILY here she had not seen before
Gemma thought, it's hard to ignore.
There were two boys she met, but yet one parent short.
There was Dad and then... that was all.

Well, SLIDE as fast as you can zoom.
SLIDE – it's the best thing to do.
Just SLIDE, go down the dips on the dunes.
It's such fun to SLIDE, can you?

They all played hide and seek, it was excellent fun!
The desert – a great place to hide.
And in turns they raced down the sand dunes in the sun,
The dad with his boys by his side.

But she needed to know and to just understand,
Since this was the reason she came,
She needed to know how this FAMILY began –
So she played the TUMMY HEART GAME!

"There is this thing I'm thinking of,
It might sound strange and funny,
But just where are your children from?
Your HEART or from your TUMMY?"

"I hope my question's not too hard,
But I'd like to know, you see,
Is your FAMILY TUMMY or HEART?
Please say if they're just like me."

Both the boys and their dad sadly looked at each other,
They hung their heads low and were quiet.
Then the dad softly said, "They did come from their mother."
Then he hugged both his boys really tight.

"See, she loved them so much though she's no longer here,"
Said the dad, in a sorrowful voice,
"But to answer your question, we'll be very clear:
A TUMMY FAMILY is our choice."

Though she liked them a lot their great answer was not
The one that she needed to hear,
So the time had now come, Gemma had to move on,
And search for that FAMILY, so dear.

As the night came around, and the air became cool,
And the stars, one-by-one, shone so bright,
It was time to move on, say goodbye to them all.
They replied, "Salaam, and goodnight."

"I'm looking for a FAMILY,
I wonder what I'll find?
I'm looking for a FAMILY
That will be just like mine."

Chapter Seven
Leaning Sideways in Italy

Next, she found a new place that served pizza so cheesy,
This country was shaped like a boot!
You're correct. It is Italy! That was quite easy!
A Ferrari drove by and did hoot!

Here she met a young girl, Francesca was her name,
And she had her own story too,
Her FAMILY had changed, it did not feel the same,
And she wasn't sure what she should do.

Well, LEAN like the tower of Pisa.
LEAN – bending down, touch your shoes.
Just LEAN sideways, and try to eat pizza.
It's fun to LEAN over, can you?

See, her mom and her dad, they still loved her so much,
But they had divorced from each other,
So then at weekends things got quite muddled up,
As she went to her dad and stepmother.

"But then where's her real mom? Wasn't she all alone?"
Are the questions I hear you ask.
She was there, she was fine and she never did moan,
She was strong enough for the task.

It was plain as can be, they both loved dear Francesca,
But things weren't as they used to be.
It is true they had changed, but for worse or for better,
They still were the same FAMILY.

But she needed to know and to just understand,
Since this was the reason she came,
She needed to know how this FAMILY began –
So she played the TUMMY HEART GAME!

"There is this thing I'm thinking of,
It might sound strange and funny,
But just where are your children from?
Your HEART or from your TUMMY?"

"I hope my question's not too hard,
But I'd like to know, you see,
Is your FAMILY TUMMY or HEART?
Please say if they're just like me."

"Though we are somewhat more complicated than most,"
Said the mom, kindly as she could,
"We're no longer together, but still we are close,
And we're TUMMY, make that understood."

Though she liked them a lot their great answer was not
The one that she needed to hear,
So the time had now come, Gemma had to move on,
And search for that FAMILY, so dear.

Gemma smiled and said "Ciao," to her new friend Francesca,
Then she climbed in a hot air balloon!
With dear Scraggs by her side, carried on her adventure,
She sang loud as she sailed past the moon.

"I'm looking for a FAMILY,
I wonder what I'll find?
I'm looking for a FAMILY
That will be just like mine."

34

Chapter Eight
Ooh La La in France

Then she landed in Paris and met a new FAMILY,
Strolling the Champs-Élysées.
A FAMILY of two dads and no mom to be seen,
They ate at a pavement café.

As she spoke with their children, they sat on a bench,
While they sketched the tall Tour Eiffel.
"We are happy to meet you, and do you speak French?
Ça va bien? That means 'are you well?'"

Well, FRENCH is a language that's fun.
FRENCH – say: *allo* and *salut*.
Fun FRENCH, *Ooh la la!* everyone!
It's fun to speak FRENCH, can you?

Oh, this FAMILY was fun, and Scraggs loved everyone.
They were all as smart as can be.
Then they walked through The Louvre, it was second to none!
There were so many things to see!

But she needed to know and to just understand,
Since this was the reason she came,
She needed to know how this FAMILY began –
So she played the TUMMY HEART GAME!

"There is this thing I'm thinking of,
It might sound strange and funny,
But just where are your children from?
Your HEART or from your TUMMY?"

"I hope my question's not too hard,
But I'd like to know, you see,
Is your FAMILY TUMMY or HEART?
Please say if they're just like me."

Both the dads looked at Gemma, and they smiled so sweet,
Then they said, "It's called surrogacy!
Our girl Charlotte is Claude's and our Pierre is Henri's,
Together, one TUMMY FAMILY!"

Though she liked them a lot their great answer was not
The one that she needed to hear,
So the time had now come, Gemma had to move on,
And search for that FAMILY, so dear.

So then Gemma moved on, as she broke into song,
And called, "*Au Revoir* and goodbye."
She'd continue her search, for she wasn't yet done
With her travels by sea, rail and sky.

"I'm looking for a FAMILY,
I wonder what I'll find?
I'm looking for a FAMILY
That will be just like mine."

Chapter Nine
Riding Elephants in India

She discovered in India a small river island,
Like no place she'd seen as of yet.
She looked out in such wonder at elephants and tigers,
Majuli – the magic islet.

Here she met with Samaira, a girl oh so cute,
And Adarsh, her big brother too.
His talent impressed her, playing tunes on his flute,
And she met with their mom, called Anu.

Well, STOMP just like an elephant.
STOMP – then slurp water too.
Just STOMP – now blow hard on your trumpet.
It's such fun to STOMP, can you?

"One more great FAMILY!" Gemma cried with a smile,
As she leapt and shouted out loud.
"With two children and Mom, on this small river isle,
No dad in this FAMILY I've found!"

But she needed to know and to just understand,
Since this was the reason she came,
She needed to know how this FAMILY began –
So she played the TUMMY HEART GAME!

"There is this thing I'm thinking of,
It might sound strange and funny,
But just where are your children from?
Your HEART or from your TUMMY?"

"I hope my question's not too hard,
But I'd like to know, you see,
Is your FAMILY TUMMY or HEART?
Please say if they're just like me."

Then mom Anu sat down and drew her children near,
Closed her eyes and thought for a while...
"We're a TUMMY FAMILY," she said, soft and sincere,
Then draped her blue sari in style.

Though she liked them a lot their great answer was not
The one that she needed to hear,
So the time had now come, Gemma had to move on,
And search for that FAMILY, so dear.

So then Gemma decided to try something fun,
And climbed on an elephant's rump.
She could sing, she could swing, it was second to none,
And Scraggs giggled with every bump.

"I'm looking for a FAMILY,
I wonder what I'll find?
I'm looking for a FAMILY
That will be just like mine."

Chapter Ten
Tick-Tock Cuckoo Clock in Switzerland

Flying high in a plane, over Alps she then snaked,
To Switzerland, so crisp and clean.
Cuckoo clocks and ski-slopes, a fountain in the lake,
With lush forests and trees so green.

Here she met a FAMILY she'd not seen anywhere,
Where the mom and the dad were away.
In this *Swiss* FAMILY, the grandparents took care
Of the twin girls, Lila and Fey.

Well, CUCKOO like a pretty Swiss clock.
CUCKOO – now move your head too.
Just CUCKOO – let your arms go tick-tock.
It's fun to CUCKOO, can you?

Oh, this FAMILY was friendly, the twins were the same,
They told Gemma "Hoy!", which means "Hi".
They all happily played 'til the end of the day,
Then they said goodnight with high-fives.

But she needed to know and to just understand,
Since this was the reason she came,
She needed to know how this FAMILY began –
So she played the TUMMY HEART GAME!

"There is this thing I'm thinking of,
It might sound strange and funny,
But just where are your children from?
Your HEART or from your TUMMY?"

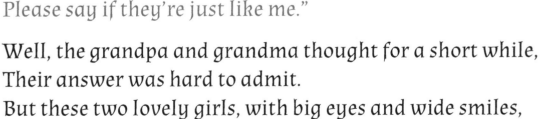

"I hope my question's not too hard,
But I'd like to know, you see,
Is your FAMILY TUMMY or HEART?
Please say if they're just like me."

Well, the grandpa and grandma thought for a short while,
Their answer was hard to admit.
But these two lovely girls, with big eyes and wide smiles,
Missed out on not one single bit.

For a reason that only the angels could know,
Mom and Dad were no longer there.
Then their Grandpa and Gran, they took over the show,
"We're a TUMMY FAMILY fair and square."

Though she liked them a lot their great answer was not
The one that she needed to hear,
So the time had now come, Gemma had to move on,
And search for that FAMILY, so dear.

Gemma bought some Swiss chocolate to take home for Dad,
And cheese fondue just for Mom.
Then she strapped on her skis and she sped down a ramp,
While she happily sang her song.

"I'm looking for a FAMILY,
I wonder what I'll find?
I'm looking for a FAMILY
That will be just like mine."

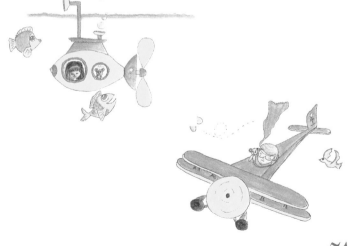

51

Chapter Eleven
Best Friends Forever in South Africa

Gemma went on her way, one more night, one more day,
And she quickly called home on her phone.
"I'm in Pretoria, Mom, I only just came,
Now, South Africa could feel like home!"

Here she found a new mom who had prayed every day,
For a daughter to call her own.
A young child she could love, who could always stay –
The sweet daughter that she'd never known.

Well, PRAY for most wonderful things,
PRAY for the moms and dads too.
Just PRAY – see what happiness brings!
It's such fun to PRAY, can you?

Now, this mom and this dad had been waiting so long
For that urgent call on the phone.
Then a lady rang up to say, "Time to be strong,
We've a child who is needing a home."

Then this mom and this dad said, "Our own little girl!"
They jumped up and down with delight.
They were bursting with joy as they both did a twirl,
"We're so happy we won't sleep tonight!"

So you see, even though this child most sweet
Was not born to them fresh and anew,
She came from their wishes, their HEARTS were complete.
This child would be perfect, they knew!

This FAMILY was magic and happy together,
Even Scraggs was delighted and eager.
Their daughter was charming and best friends with Gemma,
So finding them couldn't be sweeter!

But she needed to know and to just understand,
Since this was the reason she came,
She needed to know how this FAMILY began –
So she played the TUMMY HEART GAME!

"There is this thing I'm thinking of,
It might sound strange and funny,
But just where is your daughter from?
Your HEART or from your TUMMY?"

"I hope my question's not too hard,
But I'd like to know, you see,
Is your FAMILY TUMMY or HEART?
Please say if they're just like me."

Then the mom and the dad, they got down on their knees,
And looked Gemma right in her eyes.
Then they both proudly said, "We're a HEART FAMILY!"
Now, this was a lovely surprise!

Oh, she liked them a lot, and their answer was great.
It was just what she needed to hear.
The time had now come, Gemma's search was all done,
She had found that FAMILY, so dear!

So now just like Gemma, this little girl found
Herself with a brand new FAMILY,
In a wonderful place that was safe and was sound,
She was loved and felt so happy.

56

At first they did foster, and then they adopted.
The very best part of it yet
Was that this precious child would be safe and undaunted
And never again fear nor fret!

She has found her own place in this loving FAMILY.
They are very special indeed.
They take care and they give her all that she could need,
And that's why they're her HEART FAMILY.

So together they sang, a brand new happy song.
Gemma's search had come to an end,
And the two little girls sang out loud, sang out strong,
Delighted they'd made a new friend.

"I was looking for a FAMILY,
And look! What did I find?
I found a lovely HEART FAMILY,
A FAMILY just like mine!"

Chapter Twelve

Gemma Returns Home

Gemma's search was now done with "hellos" and "goodbyes",
Now she wanted to see Mom and Dad.
So she said her farewells with big tears in her eyes,
She and Scraggs both felt a bit sad.

Then she went on to England, back home Gemma went,
To the land of Stonehenge, Kings and Queens.
She flew over the Thames, London Eye and Big Ben,
And waved "Hi," passing Number 15.

Well, HUG your teddy so tight.
HUG – it's the best thing to do.
Just HUG – squish and squeeze him, that's right.
It's fun to bear HUG, can you?

As she opened the door, she called out with glee,
"I'm back home dear Mommy and Dad.
I belong here with you, my own HEART FAMILY,
And that makes me so very glad!"

Final Chapter
Gemma Reflects

"So tell, what is a FAMILY?
The word's bigger than the name.
And even though each one is unique,
They're really all just the same."

It does not even matter what colour they are,
If they're pink or brown; short or tall.
It does not even matter how many there are,
If the FAMILY's two, ten or four!

You see what matters most is the LOVE that they share,
The LOVE makes a FAMILY, then.
And the LOVE fills their HEARTS and then overflows when
They spread LOVE, again and again.

At the end of the day, we're all people with HEARTS.
All people, just like you and me.
And together we form our very own part
Of the GREAT BIG HUMAN FAMILY.

"I was looking for a FAMILY,
And look! What did I find?
I found a lovely HEART FAMILY,
A FAMILY just like mine!"

THE END!

Can you draw your family?

MY FAMILY.

About Barbara-Anne Puren

Having relocated to Switzerland from South Africa in September 2016 and while dealing with all of the challenges and delights that are faced when moving your entire life to another country, Barbara-Anne came to realise something profound about herself. For the greater part of her 'on stage' professional life, as an actress, singer and saxophonist, she has always thought of herself as a performance artist who writes her own material. In the last year or so, however, she has come to realise that she is rather a *writer* who performs her own material.

She has always expressed herself by writing, from one of her first poems written at 12 years of age as a reaction to seeing the words 'whites only' on a bus stop bench while growing up in apartheid South Africa, to her more recent one-woman musical stage show, *Casual Sax*, about a 40-something woman navigating the highways and byways of dating in the 21st century.

She wrote *A Family Just Like Mine* for her daughter as a way of explaining to her curious peers why she was lucky enough to have both a 'heart family' and a 'tummy family'.

www.barbarapuren.co.za

Also from Springtime Books and Summertime Publishing

Lightning Source UK Ltd.
Milton Keynes UK
UKHW051050150920
369892UK00007B/256